Cover illustration: The first unit to receive 'production' F-4Gs was the 35th TFW at George AFB, California, June 1978. These early Wild Weasels were all marked with the 'WW' tailcode regardless of their wing assignment. This example carries the then-standard ordnance for the F-4G, an AGM-45 Shrike (HARM's predecessor in the anti-radiation role) and an AGM-65 Maverick. (USAF)

1. Steam from the catapult swirls and black smoke from two J79s at full throttle fill the air as an early F-4 of VF-121 prepares to launch, May 1967. To maximize lift, all flaps on both edges of the wing are at full deflection. VF-121 wa the initial Pacific Fleet RAG (Replacement A Group) squadron for Phantoms, tasked with training replacement aircrew for the Fleet. (McDonnell Douglas)

F-4 Phantom

ROBERT C. STERN

ARMS AND ARMOUR PRESS
London—Melbourne—Harrisburg, Pa.—Cape Town

Phantom
5000th
70290

Introduction

/arbirds Illustrated 27: F-4 Phantom**
ublished in 1984 by Arms and Armour Press,
ionel Leventhal Limited, 2–6 Hampstead High
treet, London NW3 1QQ; 11 Munro Street, Port
Ielbourne 3207, Australia; Sanso Centre,
Adderley Street, P.O. Box 94, Cape Town 8000,
outh Africa; Cameron and Kelker Streets, P.O.
ox 1831, Harrisburg, Pennsylvania 17108, USA

ritish Library Cataloguing in Publication Data:
tern, Robert C.
-4 Phantom. – (Warbirds illustrated; 27)
Phantom (Fighter planes) – History – Pictorial
orks
Title II. Series
23.74′64 UG1242.F5
SBN 0–85368–670–X

diting and layout by Roger Chesneau.
ypeset by CCC, printed and bound in Great
ritain by William Clowes Limited, Beccles and
ondon.

2

. The 5,000th Phantom, an F-4E (serial number 7-290), rises vertically over the flatlands of eastern Iissouri, March 1978. It soon traded its distinctive aint scheme (two tones of blue and white) for a ore warlike finish, the colours of the Turkish Air orce. (McDonnell Douglas)

On the facing page is a photograph of a remarkable aircraft, the 5,000th McDonnell Douglas F-4 Phantom II, and along its fuselage are the flags of eleven of the twelve nations that fly F-4s. For any modern fighter to reach these milestones, in an age when each of a fighter's missiles can cost as much as a Second World War combat aircraft, is quite amazing. Yet the Phantom is an aircraft that almost never was.

The McDonnell Aircraft Company had been successful in supplying jet fighters to the US Navy since 1946, but by 1953 its future was looking rather bleak. The new F3H-1N Demon was seriously underpowered and seemed on the verge of cancellation, and the company's proposal for a Demon successor had lost to a Vought design (the F8U Crusader) in the competition to become the Navy's next-generation fighter. On its own initiative, however, McDonnell submitted a series of revised proposals in September 1953 for an entirely new single-seat, all-weather tactical fighter. Although the Navy had no current requirement for the type, the timing proved to be right: by June 1954, the Bureau of Aeronautics had evolved a tentative requirement for just such a machine, and McDonnell found itself on course for a development contract.

Nevertheless, the future was still far from bright for the new design, some inside the company feeling that the two-aircraft contract awarded in October 1954 was a sop to the loser of the big prize the year before. To compound matters, the Navy was having difficulty deciding just what role it wanted the new aircraft to play. The original designation, AH-1 (indicating an attack aircraft), was revised to become F4H-1 in June 1955 and the mission changed to fleet defence. In September, the contract for two AH-1s was replaced by one calling for five RTD&E F4H-1s, evidence of greatly increased official interest in the new project.

One more hurdle remained to be overcome, a fly-off against the F8U-3 Crusader III, but by now the Phantom's future was beginning to look more secure. However, it is doubtful that even the most optimistic at McDonnell would have dared to predict that 22 years later the 5,000th Phantom would be rolling off the assembly line or that as the design reached the age of 30 it would be a major component in the defence of the free world.

No single volume could give anything approaching complete coverage of the Phantom, but within the space available I have tried to give balanced treatment to all marks of the aircraft. Generally, I have given preference to recent views over older ones, hoping in this way to provide the reader with as many new photos as possible.

Without the help of many people and organizations, this book could never have come into existence. I would like to thank Lt. Pete Meltzer and Col. Eric Solander of the US Air Force, Rose Dyer of the McDonnell Aircraft Co., Dana Bell of NASM and, in particular, J. Erwin Jose and Ron Thurlow, who kindly opened their excellent private collections to me.

Robert C. Stern

▲3

▲4 ▼5

3. Having lost the 19 contract for the Navy' next-generation fight the McDonnell Aircra Company, at that tim delivering the first F3 Demons, set out to interest BuAer in a ne all-weather fighter design, the F3H-G. T proposed fighter, seen here in mock-up at St. Louis in May 1954, would have carried an APQ-50 radar and fou 20mm cannon and bee powered by two small Wright J65s. (McDonnell Douglas)

4. The F3H-G arouse no official interest, but when the Navy asked for proposals for an all weather attacker the same design was resubmitted under the designation AH-1. Th time there was sufficie interest for a contract for two AH-1s to be awarded to McDonne on 18 October 1954, th only change requested by BuAer being the replacement of the sma Wright jets by a pair o the big new GE J79s. I the event no AH-1s were ever built, but after almost a year of vacillation the Navy finally decided that it really needed a fleet defence interceptor more than an attacker and redesignated the AH-1 as the F4H-1 on 23 June 1955. By the time this mock-up was photographed (December 1955), the design had evolved into a recognizable Phantom. All four cannon were replaced by a quartet of new AIM-7 Sparrow air-to- air missiles, and a second crew member was added to handle the increased avionics necessitated by the new mission. (McDonnell Douglas)

5. The first F4H-1 (BuNo 142259a) nears completion on the assembly floor of McDonnell's St. Louis facility, April 1958. To the side and behind are prototype AIM-7s; the rest of the hall is full of RF-101s and F3Hs in various stages of completion. (McDonnell Douglas)

7. The first flight for
ıe Phantom prototype
ame on 27 May 1958.
'his aircraft differed
om the 1955 mock-up
ıainly in the flying
ırfaces and around the
t intakes. To protect
ainst suspected lateral
ıstability, the outer
anels of the wing were
ınted upwards and the
ıhedral already
lanned for the
ilplanes was increased.
'he jet intakes were
ılarged and the edges
ıt back from top to
ottom. The quality of
ıe design work that
ad gone into the F4H-
showed from the first
ight: pilots were
niformly enthusiastic
out its incredible
eed and power, and
rtually the only
iticism came from
ack-seaters' who
omplained of very
stricted visibility.
McDonnell Douglas)
As a general rule,
ilitary services like to
ıow off their new
rcraft, if only to
npress the taxpayers
nd their elected
presentatives, and few
ethods work better
ıan setting records.
'he US Navy was
uick to realize that the
hantom's great power
ave it the potential to
reak many of the
xisting performance
cords. In late 1959,
fter it had been
lieved of primary test
sponsibilities by the
ur remaining
TD&E airframes, the
rst Phantom was
ssigned to Project 'Top
light', an assault on
ıe world's manned
rcraft altitude record.
n 6 December it
ashed to 98,557ft,
reaking by more than
,000ft a Russian record
t the year before.
uring the testing of
arly Phantoms, some
roblems had been
ncountered with the
riginal design of the
ıtake, and in an
ttempt to improve
rflow at all speeds a
umber of different
onfigurations were
ied. Here the splitter
late has been enlarged
nd the rake in the
ıtake leading edge
iminated. (McDonnell
ouglas)

6▲

7▲ 8▼

▲9 ▼10

11▲

12▲

9. The sixth Phantom prototype (BuNo 143391) was used for initial catapult launch testing, seen here in February 1960. By this time, a second missile had been added to the Phantom's armoury, the AIM-9 Sidewinder. Because the Sidewinder is infra-red guided, an IR sensor had to be added to the Phantom's avionics suite, and an AAA-4 seeker was fitted under the radome of the F4H-1's 24in-antenna APQ-50 search radar. (McDonnell Douglas)
10. The eleventh Phantom, BuNo 145310. Of the 47 F4H-1/F-4As, 26 were assigned to test duties, the remainder going to training squadrons. Note yet another variation in splitter plate and intake leading-edge design, and also the extended cooling intake behind the radome, which replaced the NACA-style flush inlet of the earlier prototypes. (McDonnell Douglas)
11. The first squadron to receive F4H-1s was the 'Grim Reapers' of VF-101. The eleventh prototype was reassigned from RTD&E to Det A of VF-101 in 1961, the most noticeable change being the large 'AD' tailcode of the Atlantic RAG (Replacement Air Group). Aircraft 145310 is seen here in August 1961 during Operation 'Sageburner', a high-speed, low-altitude, cross-country test run from San Diego, California, to NAS Oceana, Virginia. (McDonnell Douglas)
12. The same airframe in June 1963, once again assigned to test duties. The aircraft identification marking, carried in small black lettering just in front of the tailplanes, now reads 'F-4A'. The 'rationalization' of US military aircraft nomenclature was just one of Robert McNamara's many controversial achievements as President John F. Kennedy's Secretary of Defense. (McDonnell Douglas)

AD
NAVY
184
DANGER

▲13 ▼14

JET
STEP
DANGER
PULL HANDLE TO JETTISON CANOPIES
INTAKE
RESCUE
CAUTION
USE DURING MAINTENANCE ONLY

3. As late as the early 1960s air races were still major events in
e US, none bigger than the Bendix Trophy races held at
ntario, California. The US Navy and USAF would regularly
nd teams of their latest and hottest aircraft to compete in the
ilitary-class races. This F4H-1F (BuNo 148268a, from the last
oduction batch of F-4As) of VF-101 Det A, seen at the 1961
endix race on 21 May of that year, shows most of the features
at were to become standard on the F-4B. It is marked with large
ternational orange bands behind the radome and on the fuselage
d belly tank. (US Navy)

4. An early F-4B in front of the manufacturer's hangar at
ambert Field, St. Louis, June 1960. The F-4B differed from the
 in several respects: a larger radar, the 32in-diameter APQ-72
troduced on a few F-4As, became standard, along with the
quisite larger radome; the back seat was raised; and the entire
nopy design was altered to give better forward vision for both
ewmen. However, the intake design seen here is not the ultimate
rsion introduced during the -B model run. F-4Bs were also
ted with uprated engines, J79-GE-8s, in place of the -A's -2s.
McDonnell Douglas)

5. One early F-4B (BuNo 149449) was assigned the task of
eaking the world's time-to-climb records in Project 'High
Jump', and during April 1962 this standard aircraft set new
records at all eight recognized height increments between 3,000
and 30,000m, reaching the latter altitude in 371.43 seconds. The
Phantom's records proved enduring: the five lower altitude
records were not broken until early 1975, when they fell to the F-15 Streak Eagle. (McDonnell Douglas)

16. Early F-4Bs were immediately assigned to fill out the fleet's
training squadrons. Here a pair of F-4Bs (BuNo 148419 is in the
foreground) of VF-121's 'Pacemakers', the Pacific RAG
squadron, fly over La Jolla, California, on 26 April 1962. The
Phantom in the foreground is marked with a yellow lightning bolt
and a black cat; markings of this complexity are fairly rare among
RAG 'birds', which are more often as plain as the F-4B in the
background. (US Navy)

17. As soon as they became available, new F-4Bs were delivered to
the Fleet. The famous 'Pukin' Dogs' of VF-143 were among the
first fleet squadrons to re-equip with the Phantom, BuNo 150443
being seen here after having caught a wire on board *Constellation*,
28 June 1963. The winged dog on the fuselage is black; the
tailstripe with four white 'Pukin' Dog' silhouettes is blue; and
'NK' identifies CVW-14. (US Navy)

15▼

16▼

17▼

▲18

18. The 'Jolly Rogers' of CVW-7's VF-84 were anothe early conversion to F-4Bs. Note the different lengths of the nose oleo strut of these tw aircraft. The F-4's nose landing gear could be extende by the pilot to raise the nose and increase alpha for take off and landing. (McDonnell Douglas)

19. Another early fleet conversion was by CVW-17 o board *Forrestal*. F-4Bs of both of that wing's fighter squadrons can be seen here, VF-74 with yellow trim in the foreground and VF-11 with red trim on the catapult. (US Navy via Dana Bell)

20. CAG (Commander Air Group) machines are always the most colourful. Traditionally they carry the number '100' (or sometimes just '00' – 'Double Nuts') and tail decoration with the colou of each of air wing's squadron CVW-1's seven component squadrons are represented by an equal number of stripes on CAG-1's rudder. Equally traditionally, the CAG 'bird' a fighter (in this case an F-4B BuNo 149448) carrying the markings of the wing's senior fighter squadron (in this case the 'Tophatters' of VF-14, 29 July 1964). (US Navy)

21. As more advanced Phantom variants took over squadron duties from F-4Bs, many of the early airframes were assigned to various test programmes. Here an F-4B-8 MC (BuNo 148412h) of VFX 1 is shown during testing of th Phoenix missile system, September 1968. An XAIM-54A is being carried in a speci centreline pod designed to simulate the semi-recessed Phoenix mounting on the F-1 Tomcat. (McDonnell Douglas)

22. Some of the Phantoms assigned to test squadrons hav become famous for their colo schemes. The third F-4B (BuNo 148365) is seen here a a QF-4B drone controller (no the extra antennae behind the radome) belonging to the Naval Missile Command, Jun 1978. Painted overall international orange, it soon earned the nickname 'Iron Butterfly'. (McDonnell Douglas)

◀19

20▲

21▲ 22▼

▲23

▲24

23. The RF-4B was actually the second photo reconnaissance version of the Phantom, being a standard F-4B fitted with the nose developed for the Air Force's F-4C. The first RF-4B (BuNo 151975t) is seen here in March 1965. Photo Phantoms exchanged the large APQ-72 for a smaller APQ-99 radar optimized for navigation and a variety of sensors including forward-looking, side-looking and/or downward-looking cameras (the camera mountings are designed to be capable of modification in the field according to tactical requirements), side-looking radar, infra-red sensors and a laser reconnaisance system. (McDonnell Douglas)

24. An RF-4B (BuNo 153105) of VMFP-3 on board *Midway*, camouflaged in the overall gull grey scheme adopted in the 1970s. As part of an overall sensor upgrade programme undertaken by the Marines during the late 1970s, in an attempt to extend the service life of its RF-4Bs through to the 1980s, this photo Phantom has received the small RHAWS (Radar Homing and Warning System) sensors on either side of its nose and an integrated ECM fairing behind each main intake.

25. Inter-service rivalry in the USA is legendary, and it is with the greatest reluctance that one service accepts an aircraft originally developed by another. The fine qualities of the Phantom, however, and the serious need of the Air Force for a state-of-the-art tactical fighter, led that service to 'borrow' a pair of F-4Bs for evaluation. Both are seen here at Lambert Field, St. Louis, prior to their delivery to TAC headquarters at Langley AFB, January 1962. The original Air Force designation was F-110A. In the foreground is the first of the pair, retaining its Navy serial (BuNo 149405), carried USAF-style minus its first digit on the tail. This aircraft was later redesignated F-4C (USAF)

26. The buzz number code assigned to the Phantom was 'FJ', as can be seen here on the underside of the first Air Force F-4, January 1962. A buzz number – a large identification number on the aircraft's belly – was supposed to discourage the 'buzzing' of civilians (low-altitude overflights), each aircraft type having a different code sequence. (McDonnell Douglas)

27. The Air Force was forced to acknowledge that the Phantom outflew anything it had or was planning, and reached agreement with the Navy to take 27 more F-4Bs off McDonnell's assembly line, all to be redesignated F-4C. Before the Air Force could begin to acquire large numbers of Phantoms, however, a series of changes to the basic F-4B had to be implemented to make the Phantom more suitable for land-based service. These included the adoption of larger, low-pressure mainwheel tyres (necessitating the thickening of the wing root) and the fitting of full dual controls and cartridge starters. The Navy-style retractable refuelling probe was replaced by a receptacle behind the cockpit for USAF-style boom refuelling. The fourth 'real' F-4C (63-7410) is seen here on 27 January 1964, test-firing an AGM-12B Bullpup (which was intended to be one of the Air Force Phantom's prime weapons). (USAF)

25▲

26▲ 27▼

▲28 ▼29

3. An early Air Force
xercise involving
hantoms was 'Goldfire
', held at Fort Leonard
Vood, Missouri, in
October 1964. This F-
C (63-7426) carries a
road blue band
iagonally across the
ear fuselage for the
xercise. (USAF)
9. F-4Cs were heavily
ommitted to combat in
ietnam (as were Navy
hantoms). Here 63-
647, an F-4C of the 8th
FW 'Wolfpack',
fuels from a KC-135
n route to a MiGCAP
ission over Hanoi.
ote the red star on the
litter plate, indicating
previous victory over a
MiG. Aerial combat
ith the older, slower
ut more agile MiGs
howed up the
isadvantages inherent
the Phantom's all-
issile armament and
its large size. While
othing could be done
make the Phantom
ny smaller, most later
hanges to the breed
ere aimed at resolving
hese problems.
USAF)
0. Rapidly
pproaching their 20th
irthday, most F-4Cs
63-7420 is seen here in
eptember 1979) have
isappeared from
egular' TAC service,
emaining only with
aining units such as
he 310th TFTS, 58th
FTW, Luke AFB,
rizona.
1. Gradually over the
ast decade, F-4Cs
iscarded by TAC took
ver from even older F-
01s in Air National
Guard units assigned to
ADCOM (Aerospace
Defense Command),
iving up their tactical
amouflage in favour of
ADCOM's overall grey
cheme. Aircraft 64-952
as assigned to the
orth Dakota ANG's
19th FIG, the 'Happy
Hooligans', and is seen
ere on 30 August 1979.
USAF)
2. Many ex-TAC
-4Cs, like 64-942 of
NDANG's 119th FIG,
ot their three-colour
amouflage back again
hen ADCOM was
bsorbed by TAC,
ecoming ADTAC.
The 'ribbon' on the tail
f this F-4C indicates
hat it is a veteran of
ietnam. (USAF)

30▲

31▲ 32▼

▲33

33. The YRF-4C (62-12200) was the original photo-reconnaissance Phantom, first flying in 1963. This airframe, after its days as the primary recon test-bed were over, would reappear as the YF-4E and more. (USAF via Dana Bell)

34. Protected by steel revetments against Viet Cong mortar attacks, early RF-4Cs are here parked at Tan Son Nhut Air Base, Vietnam. Modern air defence environments, such as were encountered in South-East Asia, make tactical reconnaisance by platforms with any less performance than the Phantom almost suicidal. (USAF)

35▲

Since the Air Force has not developed a reconnaissance rsion of F-15, the RF-4C remains very much in evidence in nt-line squadrons. Aircraft 65-940, part of the 18th TFW based Kadena Air Base, Japan, is seen here at Clark AB, the ilippines, during 'Cope Thunder 80'; the 18th has since converted to F-15s. This RF-4C has been modernized with the new, more streamlined nose developed for the RF-4E. It may be noted, incidentally, that the US Navy has not developed a new recon aircraft either, but has begun deployment of TARPS-equipped F-14s to replace Marine RF-4Bs. (Ron Thurlow)

▲36

▲37 ▼38

39▲

36. The special paint scheme on its tail, in place of the normal 'RR' tailcode, indicates that this RF-4C (66-422) belongs to the 38th TRS, 26th TRW, based at Ramstein AB, West Germany. (J. Erwin Jose)

37. Aircraft of the 32nd TRS, 10th TRW, based at RAF Alconbury, carry an 'AT' tailcode; the wing is noted for the variety of decoration on its aircraft. This RF-4C (66-433) has a cartoon Phantom on its splitter plate and a caricature of a beer-drinking German on its nose. (J. Erwin Jose)

38. The 'AR' tailcode denotes aircraft of the blue-tailstriped 1st TRS, 10th TRW, also based at RAF Alconbury. Here an RF-4C (68-556) lands at that station, trailing its yellow drag 'chute behind it. (J. Erwin Jose)

39. Taxying in after landing (note the open drag 'chute compartment at the tail), this 1st TRS RF-4C (65-944) has the new, more aerodynamic, RF-4E-style nose. (J. Erwin Jose)

40. A close-up view of the nose of 'Freeze Frame', a shark-mouthed RF-4C (of the 26th TRW, seen at Spangdahlem AB, West Germany, 1983), provides a good look at the new nose contours and the port-side RHAWS sensor. A small, black cartoon of the Phantom can be seen on the cooling intake, with the legends 'I Spy' and 'Mox Nix'. An increasing number of USAF units are experimenting with 'wraparound' camouflage, as shown here. (J. Erwin Jose)

40▼

▲41

▲42 ▼43

ɫ. An F-4D banks
ver the seemingly
ndless forest of
ietnam. The -D
iffered from the F-4C
xternally only in
aving a slightly larger
ose cross-section, in
rder to house the new
PQ-109 radar with its
nproved air-to-ground
apability. A new
eapons release
omputer and 30kVA
enerator occupied the
orward fuselage fuel
ell, reducing fuel
apacity and range
ccordingly.
McDonnell Douglas)
2. F.4Ds can still be
ound in front-line
nits, though they are
arting to become rare:
th TFW F-4Ds (for
xample 66-8805, seen
ere landing at Kunsan
B, Korea, in 1979),
ave recently been
eplaced by F-16s. Note
e LORAN antenna on
e Phantom's spine.
USAF)

3. An F-4D (65-681)
f the 3rd TFW lands at
orat AB, Thailand,
aving flown in from
lark AB as part of
peration 'Commando
crimmage', 11 March
975. The 'JJ' tailcode
as now been replaced
y 'PN' and the F-4Ds
ave given way to F-
Es. (USAF)
4. An 81st TFW F-4D
65-696) taxies out at
AF Woodbridge. To
ake up for the lack of
un armament, F-4Ds
ften carry a 20mm gun
od on the centreline.
J. Erwin Jose)
5. A pair of F-4Ds of
e 81st TFW take off
om Woodbridge, July
978. Both of these
hantoms carry an AN/
LQ-119 ECM pod
nder the forward
uselage. Effective ECM
considered an
bsolute necessity over
urope today. (J. Erwin
ose)
6. A red-tailstriped F-
D (66-7768) of the
01st TFW from
orrejon, Spain, at
amstein AB, West
ermany, 1979. (J.
rwin Jose)

44▲

45▲ 46▼

▲47

▲48 ▼49

47. Another USAFE unit to operate F-4Ds was the 52nd TFW, based at Spangdahlem AB, West Germany. This F-4D-30-MC (6 7527), armed with an AGM-65 Maverick, is seen at Bitburg AB, 1979. (J. Erwin Jose)
48. The 50th TFW at Hahn AB, West Germany, also operate F-4Ds during the 1970 This cannon-armed -D (65-763) of the 496th TFS is seen on the taxiway at Hahn. (J. Erwin Jose)
49. The final USAF unit to fly D-model Phantoms was the 36th TFW at Bitburg AB, West Germany: this F-4D-31-MC is aircraft 77-7705 of the 53rd TFS. The 36th TFW became the first USAF unit to operate F-15 Eagles. (J. Erwin Jose)
50. Gaudy in its international orange tes markings and carrying load of 24 equally brigh Mk 82 500lb GP bombs an early Phantom (F4H-1F, BuNo 145310) is seen in flight during weapons carriage testing in April 1961. (McDonnell Douglas)
51. An F-4B (BuNo 150642) prepares to launch from an unidentified aircraft carrier in July 1966; the camouflage, medium green over white, is obviously experimental. Many of the Phantoms from the same production batch (F-4B-14-MCs) went to the Air Force as the original F-4Cs, and this Navy machine carries the bureau number on its tail in the style of an Air Force serial number. (McDonnell Douglas)
52. (Next spread) Its nosewheel leg extended, an F-4B (BuNo 151506) of VF-84 (USS *Independence*) awaits launch off *Saratoga*'s starboard catapult, October 1964. Note the raised blast screen behind the Phantom, intended to protect waiting aircraft from hot exhaust, and also the VF-101 Phantom in the background waiting to assume its position on the port catapult. (McDonnell Douglas)

50▲ 51▼

209
A G

200
DANGER
INTAKE
AD
143

▲53

▲54 ▼55

. An RF-4C (64-1019) of
: 192nd TRG, Nevada
JG, in flight over the Canal
ne, 8 August 1979. Since no
wer tactical reconnaissance
craft has been developed by
: Air Force, Air Guard
oto Phantoms like this
uld probably play a
ominent part in any future
nflict. (USAF)

. A pair of 'Wolfpack' F-
)s (66-7531 is in the
eground) bank over the
mlands of South Korea.
ke many front-line Air Force
its equipped with early
antoms, the 8th TFW has
ven up its F-4s for newer
signs, in this case for F-16s.
ote the PACAF badge on the
rtical tail. (USAF)

. Out for a day of ACM (Air
mbat Manoeuvres) training
e a shark-mouthed F-4E (71-
76) of the 3rd TFW and an
5E of the 26th TFTAS
'actical Fighter Training
ggressor Squadron), both
sed at Clark AFB, the
ilippines, 22 January 1981.
the time of writing, the 3rd
mains the only full wing in
ACAF still flying Phantoms.
JSAF)

. F-4Ds also equipped a
all number of CONUS
Continental US) TAC units
til the late 1970s. The 42nd
FW at Eglin AFB, Florida,
s now switched over to F-
s, but when this photograph
as taken (5 May 1970) it was
ll completely equipped with
antoms. This F-4D (66-
17) carries a pair of QRC-
5-3 ECM pods and, judging
om the tailband design,
gmented in three parts, is
ost likely the wing CO's
rsonal mount. (USAF via
ana Bell)

. A quartet of F-4Ds of the
4th TFS, 4th TFW, based at
ymour-Johnson AFB, North
arolina, stands at alert. In the
reground is 66-7710, an F-
)-31-MC. 'Alert birds' are
elled and ready to taxi;
arly all CONUS fighter units
ve alert responsibility for
me section of the US border.
JSAF via Dana Bell)

. An F-4D (66-7667) of the
'4th TFW, based at Nellis
FB in Nevada, lands in the
te afternoon, silhouetted
ainst the mountains of the
gh desert and with its drag
hute trailing behind. It is
rticipating in Operation
Black Fury III', January 1980.
JSAF)

56▲

57▲ 58▼

▲59

▲60 ▼61

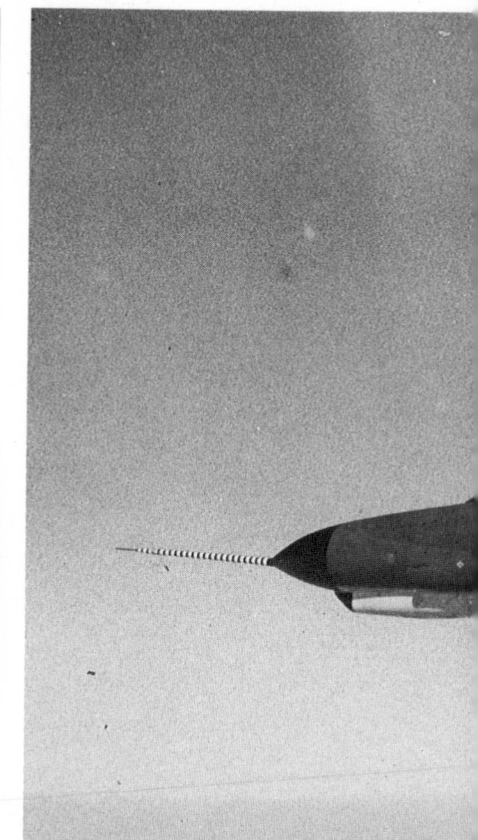

59. The lack of an integral gun armament, belatedly and only partially resolved by the development of a gun pod, led early on to the idea of developing a version of the F-4 with an internal mounting for a 20mm rotary cannon (Gatling gun). Besides the ubiquitous 62-12200, which became the 'official' YF-4E, a number of -Cs and -Ds were experimentally fitted with what was to become the production -E nose. Such was the case with this F-4C (63-7445), seen at Edwards AFB, California, during testing of the FIGAT (Fibre Glass Aerial Target), 24 March 1971. The -E nose incorporated the smaller-diameter APQ-120 radar in order to make room for the barrels of the 20mm cannon, which fired from beneath the nose. (USAF)

60. Another earlier Phantom modified into an F-4E test-bed was this ex-F-4D (65-713), seen with a pair of CBU-34/As (cluster bomb units) under each wing, July 1969. This particular airframe was also being used to test a rudder containing a large percentage of boron in an attempt to save weight. (USAF via Dana Bell)

61. The actual YF-4E (ex-YRF-4C, s/n 62-12200) never carried the production -E nose: it simply had the cameras removed from its sensor compartment and replaced by the cannon which fired through the resulting gap. Following the completion of its duties as an -E test-bed, the YF-4E was again modified as the test airframe for Project 'Agile Eagle' in June 1969. This involved the fitting of extendable manoeuvring slats in place of the blown wing leading-edge flaps then standard on F-4s. All production F-4Es had the fixed leading-edge slots on the tailplane originally developed by the Navy for its contemporary F-4J in an effort to keep down landing speeds as the Phantom's gross weight increased. Like the modified F-4D seen in the last photograph, the YF-4E had a rudder largely made out of light metal, in this case beryllium. All light metals like boron and beryllium present significant manufacturing problems and they were never seriously considered for series production. In the 1980s, composite materials have emerged as a much more practical solution to the problem of saving weight in aircraft. (McDonnell Douglas)

62. The second production F-4E (66-285) was modified for use in stall tests by the extension of its tail fairing to house a pair of large parachutes. These tests were necessitated by the new slotted tailplane and the fitting of more powerful J-79-GE-17s, distinguished by longer afterburner vanes. Aircraft '285' is seen here at Edwards AFB, 1 March 1970. The tail is overall international orange and the undersurfaces of the wing outer panels carry large orange stripes. (USAF)

62▼

▲63 ▼64

◀65

63. The F-4E remains in service with a large number of front-line units. Many, like 68-493 of the 3rd TFW seen here landing at its home base (Clark AB, the Philippines), are veterans of the Vietnam War and recorded victories during that conflict: note the red star on the splitter plate. Most F-4Es still flying have been retrofitted with the leading-edge slats tried out on the YF-4E; at the same time, most had an extended fairing fitted to the cannon muzzle housing. Many current Phantom pilots have been flying for far fewer years than their mounts. (USAF)

64. Ground crewmen of the 3rd TFW bring out an AN/ALQ-119 ECM pod to a line-up of F-4Es during 'Team Spirit 79', an annual joint exercise held with the ROKAF, Osan AB, South Korea, 6 March 1979. The AN/ALQ-119, which has undergone a constant change of configuration, is the most common ECM pod carried by F-4s. (USAF)

65. A limited number of F-4Es have had a TISEO (Target Identification System, Electro-Optical) TV camera fitted to the leading edge of the port wing, as on this 3rd TFW F-4E, seen at 'Team Spirit 79'. TISEO projects a magnified TV image in the rear cockpit, allowing BVR (beyond visual range) target identification. (USAF)

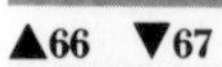
▲66 ▼67

66, 67, 68. 'Bataan', the personal F-4E (68-312) of the CO of the 3rd TFW. The serial on the tail has been modified in non-standard fashion to identify the unit, whilst the nearby badge is PACAF's; as is customary for a wing CO's aircraft, the tailstripes of all three component squadrons (red, red-white-blue and light blue) are combined. The nose marking is a map of Luzon, the main Philippine island, where Clark AB and the Bataan Peninsula (of Bataan Death March fame) are both located. (Ron Thurlow)

68▼

69. A red-tailstriped F-4E (72-165) of the 50th TFW lands in front of parked Transalls at Jever AB, West Germany, during the annual Tactical Air Meet held there, in 1981. The leading-edge slats have already been retracted on this modified -E but their presence is indicated by the triple actuator fairings under each wing. (J. Erwin Jose)

70. Considerable doubt as to the ability of the F-16 to handle Europe's often atrocious weather conditions has led to a reluctance on the part of USAFE to give up its trusty F-4s before the F-16 proves itself. The white-tailstriped 313th TFS of the 50th TFW was the first unit to begin the transition to Falcons in 1982. Aircraft 68-384 is an F-4E of the 313th, seen here at Hahn AB in April 1981. Other Phantom units in USAFE are scheduled to follow the lead of the 50th TFW, should their experience prove successful. (J. Erwin Jose)

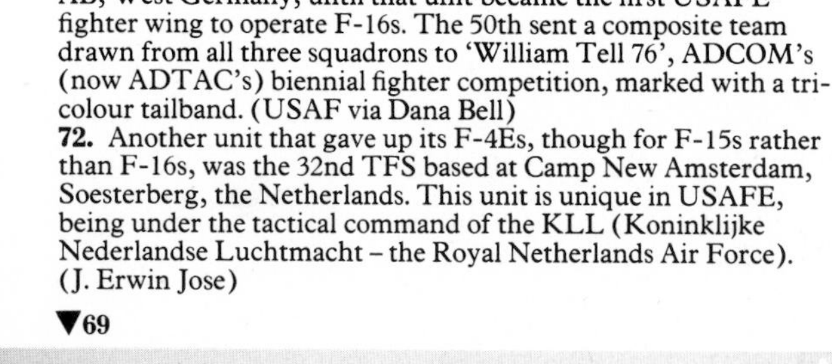

71. Three squadrons of F-4Es made up the 50th TFW at Hahn AB, West Germany, until that unit became the first USAFE fighter wing to operate F-16s. The 50th sent a composite team drawn from all three squadrons to 'William Tell 76', ADCOM's (now ADTAC's) biennial fighter competition, marked with a tri-colour tailband. (USAF via Dana Bell)

72. Another unit that gave up its F-4Es, though for F-15s rather than F-16s, was the 32nd TFS based at Camp New Amsterdam, Soesterberg, the Netherlands. This unit is unique in USAFE, being under the tactical command of the KLL (Koninklijke Nederlandse Luchtmacht – the Royal Netherlands Air Force). (J. Erwin Jose)

▼69

▼70

71▲ 72▼

▲73

73. The next USAFE unit scheduled to receive F-16s is the F-4E-equipped 86th TFW based at Ramstein AB, West Germany. This red and black chequerboard-tail F-4E, 74-657, of the 536th TFS, is about to be lifted at its four hoist points by a mobile airfield crane. Note the yellow plastic cover over the wing leading-edge TISEO sensor. (J. Erwin Jose)

74. This sharkmouthed, yellow and black chequerboard-tail F-4 (68-378) of the 526th TFS, 86th TFW, seen at Ramstein AB, Jul 1980, carries a large yellow 'B' on its tail as a temporary tactical marking. (J. Erwin Jose)

▼74

75▲

. A Maverick-equipped F-4E (68-490) of the 86th TFW, arked with a yellow tailstripe, in front of a concrete blast shelter Ramstein AB, 1981. To protect against the devastation of ATO air power on the ground by a surprise strike, more and ore USAFE aircraft are being housed in covered revetments like is. (J. Erwin Jose)

. The 52nd TFW operates three squadrons of F-4Es (such as aircraft 72-124 of the 480th TFS, seen here in June 1980) from Spangdahlem AB, West Germany. This wing is known for its recent camouflage experiments. This TISEO-equipped Phantom uses the standard colours of the Vietnam-era camouflage (two greens and tan over pale grey) but in non-standard proportions, using less tan. (J. Erwin Jose)

76▼

▲77

78▲

◀79

77. A sharkmouthed F-4E (74-1650, of the 52nd TFW), at the International Air Tattoo, RAF Greenham Common, in 1983. It is painted in the European I scheme, known popularly as 'Charcoal Lizard' and originally designed for A-10s. It is composed of two tones of green and charcoal grey, carried around on all surfaces. (E. deKruyff via J. Erwin Jose)

78. Based in Iceland but part of ADTAC rather than USAFE (hence the overall grey paint scheme), is the 57th FIS at Keflavik AB, 1980. The black and white chequerboard tail on this F-4E (66-382) is traditional with the 57th. The knight's helmet insignia on the nose is derived from the squadron's badge. (J. Erwin Jose)

79. The same F-4E at the International Air Tattoo, RAF Greenham Common, in 1983. The knight's helmet has disappeared from the nose and unit badges have been applied to the splitter plate and intake. (E. deKruyff via J. Erwin Jose)

▲80

80. A number of 'stateside' TAC units regularly operate from European bases in order to familiarize themselves with the terrain and weather they would be likely to encounter should diplomacy fail. One such unit is the 4th TFW, based at Seymour-Johnson AFB, South Carolina; the 'SJ' tailcode replaces that unit's former 'SA' code. This 4th TFW F-4E (72-1479) is seen on 5–6 October 1978 at Ramstein, during Exercise 'Autumn Forge'. (USAF)

81. Another F-4E (66-293) of the 4th TFW, at Ramstein in 1980. One recent trend, even among squadrons retaining standard camouflage, has been the use of black rather than white or pale grey paint for the tail markings. This old aircraft is the tenth production -E. (Ron Thurlow)

82. Another CONUS TAC unit often seen on overseas deployment is the 347th TFW, Moody AFB, Georgia. This unit has been chosen repeatedly to participate in joint US-Egyptian exercises, such as 'Proud Phantom', July 1980. Here a pair of the 347th's F-4Es (68-431 is to the left) are seen in front of a hardened shelter at Cairo-West AB, Egypt. (USAF)

81▲ 82▼

▲83

83. A pair of F-4Es, 67-360 from the 347th TFW and 66-366 of the Egyptian Air Force, in front of one of the Great Pyramids at Giza during 'Bright Star', a major all-arms tactical exercise held in March 1982. (McDonnell Douglas)

84. The same Egyptian F-4E (66-366), this time over the Western Desert in November 1980, wearing a two-tone grey camouflage similar in pattern to USAF's Vietnam camouflage. The Egyptians have considered selling their 35 F-4Es to Turkey (which also operates -Es) now that they are purchasing F-16s, but recent experience during their near-perennial hostility with Libya has encouraged them to retain their Phantoms for the moment. Like most other non-US Phantoms, the Egyptian F-4Es are ex-USAF airframes refurbished by McDonnell Douglas for their ne owners. (McDonnell Douglas)

85. A Wild Weasel Phantom (F-4G, ex-F-4E, 69-7234) of the 35th TFW based at George AFB, California, seen at Nellis AFB, Nevada, in May 1980. The aircraft is fitted with an AGM-78 Standard ARM, an anti-radiation derivative of the surface-to-ai RIM-66A Standard Missile 1 carried on board virtually every U Navy ship. (USAF)

86. An F-4G (ex-F-4E, 69-7546) of the 563rd TFS, 37th TFW, scrambles from a concrete revetment at RAF Wildenrath shortly after dawn, October 1982, during Exercise 'Reforger 82'. The 37th is based at George AFB, California. (USAF)

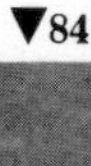
▼84

85▲ 86▼

▲87 ▼88

89▲

87. An F-4G of the 563rd TFS, 37th TFW, banks over lush terrain somewhere in West Germany during Exercise 'Reforger 82', October 1982. (USAF)
88. A pair of F-4Ns of VF-201 ('Hunters') at NAS Dallas, March 1983. The aircraft on the left is in the older overall gull grey scheme; that on the right is painted in the new three-tone tactical scheme.
89. Perhaps the most colourful Phantom, at least in US markings, was this Bicentennial example, an F-4S of VX-4 based at NAS Miramar, California, a unit noted for its exotic paint schemes. The photograph was taken in June 1978. (McDonnell Douglas)

▲90 ▼91

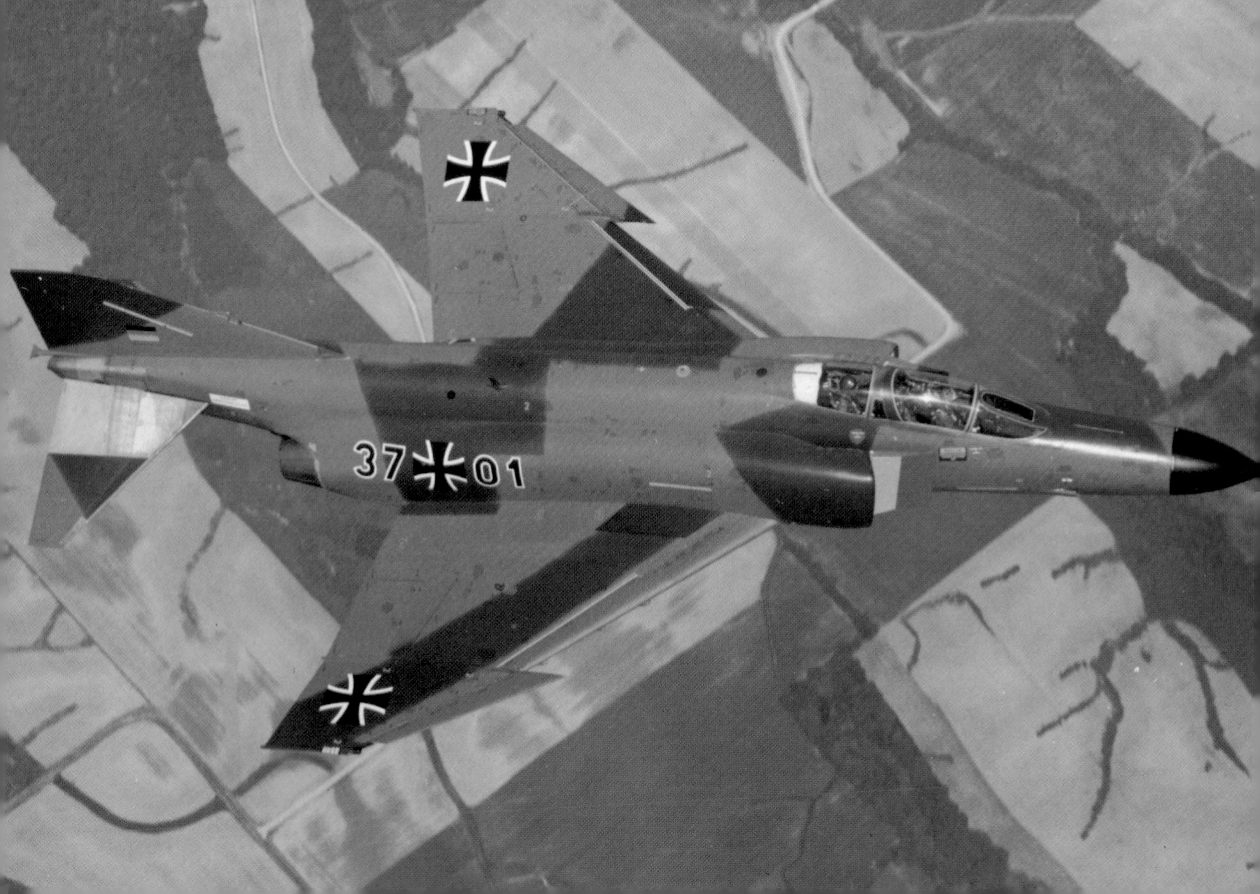

92▲

). VX-4's most famous F-4 is its 'Playboy Phantom', now an F-
S (BuNo 155539), painted overall glossy black with the famed
layboy magazine bunny on its tail. NAS Dallas, March 1983.
1. The first F-4F, essentially an F-4E built to West German
ecifications and incorporating a high percentage of German-
uilt sub-assemblies, is seen over the flatlands of Missouri in May
)73. All F-4Fs were built at St. Louis for economic reasons.
McDonnell Douglas)
2. The RF-4E was developed by McDonnell Douglas and the
'S Air Force for export only, to meet the tremendous demand for
fective tactical reconnaissance. A total of 130 aircraft were
dered by five nations, although 16 of Iran's order for 28 were
ter cancelled after the overthrow of the Shah. 'Spirit of St.
Louis', the first RF-4E (69-7448; 35+01 of the Luftwaffe) is
shown here on 20 January 1971.
93. For the West Germans, McDonnell Douglas built a variant of
the F-4E with two MTU-built J79-GE-17As (and other West
German sub-assemblies), no slots on the tailplane, no provision
for AIM-7 Sparrows and a reduced fuel capacity. One hundred
and seventy-five of these F-4Fs were built at St. Louis, including
38+36 of JaG 74 'Molders' seen here. This airframe carried the
USAF serial 72-1246 – all military aircraft built in the US, even
those built to foreign order and design, carry a US military serial
number; hence the only Phantoms never to do so were those built
in other countries, specifically the F-4EJs assembled in Japan. (J.
Erwin Jose)

93▼

94. A new, streamlined sensor nose was developed during the RF-4E production run and later retrofitted to many RF-4Cs. This RF-4E (75-419), in USAF markings in March 1977, was built for delivery to Israel. It is painted in the two-tone ghost grey air-superiority camouflage scheme used on F-15s. (McDonnell Douglas)
95. The JASDF (Japanese Air Self Defence Force – Koku Jieitai) developed its own versions of the F-4E and RF-4E. This RF-4EJ (47-6902), October 1974, is painted in a pale grey over white camouflage. The first two F-4EJs were built by McDonnell Douglas, but all the remaining 138 were assembled in Japan by Mitsubishi; all 20 RF-4EJs, however, were built at St. Louis. (McDonnell Douglas)

94▶

95▼

96. The US Navy continued to develop the Phantom in parallel with the Air Force. The F-4J (BuNo 155575 is shown at St. Louis in March, 1968) actually preceded the F-4E off the McDonnell Douglas assembly line. It was powered by J79-GE-8Bs, -8Cs or -10s, of similar static thrust (17,900lb) to the -E's -17s, and was the first mark of Phantom to be equipped with the slotted tailplane, intended to help reduce the -J's landing speed, which otherwise would have been significantly too high owing to the aircraft's increased gross weight. F-4Js also carried the more advanced APG-59 radar and the AWG-10 fire control system. This latter took over the forward fuselage fuel bay, as on the F-4D, but the Navy was unwilling to accept reduced capacity and added a new tank under the vertical tail which actually resulted in a net increase in the Phantom's internal fuel storage. To simplify production, the F-4J adopted the larger mainwheels and thickened wing root introduced on the F-4C. (McDonnell Douglas)

97. F-4Js began replacing the oldest of the F-4Bs in fleet squadrons as soon as they became available. Here BuNo 157257 of the 'Aardvarks' (VF-114) prepares to launch from *Kitty Hawk* on 7 April 1975 during Operation 'Rimpac 75', a joint exercise with Canada, Australia and New Zealand. Note the ECM fairing on the outside of the main intake; nearly all F-4Js carry such faired ECM pods, in various styles, on both sides. (US Navy)

96▲ 97▼

▲98 ▼99

100▲

98. A pair of F-4Js of VF-11's 'Red Rippers' (BuNo 157276 is in the background) on board *Forrestal* in June 1976. Note the Bicentennial marking on the fuselage and the coveted 'Battle E' on the splitter plate. (US Navy)
99. The launch officer gives the 'thumbs up' to VMFA-33's CO as he prepares to launch off *Nimitz*'s waist catapult, November 1976. The markings of the 'Fighting Shamrocks' F-4Js are green and white; a Phantom of CVW-8's other fighter squadron is parked immediately astern. (US Navy)
100. Along with the boar's head of the 'Red Rippers', one of the Navy's oldest squadron insignia is 'Felix the Cat', now carried by VF-31. Aircraft 153891 is taxying at NAS Roosevelt Roads, Puerto Rico, on 20 July 1979. VF-31 was part of *Saratoga*'s air wing. The markings are red, black and white. (US Navy)
101. An F-4J of VF-151 (BuNo 153841) prepares for launch from *Midway*'s port catapult in choppy seas. F-4Js, along with F-4Es, incorporated 'drooping ailerons' which could be depressed when the flaps were at full deflection to provide extra lift during take off and landing. The fairing on the forward edge of the rear canopy houses a rear-view mirror intended to help the 'bear' (the rear-seater) 'clear Six'. VF-151's markings were black and yellow tailstripes.

101▼

▲102

102. VF-101's 'Grim Reapers' were still the Atlantic Fleet RAG squadron for Phantoms in the late 1970s, although now it flew F-4Js; 155568 is shown, at NAS Oceana. The tailcode was still 'AD', but the markings were much more colourful, including red, white and blue tailstripes and a red and yellow 'Grim Reapers' badge on the fuselage. (Dana Bell)

103. A quartet of some of the most colourful Phantoms ever to fly in formation, two F-4Bs and two F-4Js of VX-4, the Navy's west coast experimental squadron based at NAS Miramar, California, June 1978. The lead aircraft is an F-4J (BuNo 153783) in one of the many incarnations of the 'Playboy Phantom', all black witl white markings. The trailing aircraft is the same 'Iron Butterfl QF-4B seen in illustration 22. The other two are a -B and a -J painted in experimental camouflage, the former in overall air superiority blue (except for white radome), tried out and rejec by the Air Force for its F-15 prototypes, and the latter in two tones of light blue in a broad-striped pattern. The Navy has generally adopted new camouflage for the 1980s, but it is neith of these patterns. (McDonnell Douglas)

▼103

104▲

)4. The Air Force's experience over Hanoi, in the densest air efence environment yet created, proved the need for aircraft edicated to the suppression of anti-air weapons and sensors: ıese emerged first as field-modified F-105 Wild Weasels and later factory-converted F-105Gs. By 1975, the Air Force had begun riously to consider using newer and faster Phantoms in the place the war-weary 'Thuds' in the Wild Weasel role, and one of the rst experimental conversions was this F-4D (65-713, which had reviously been converted to F-4E configuration – see photo 60), seen here on 20 August 1975 with a load of CBUs. (USAF)

105. Late in 1975 several F-4Es were converted into F-4G Advanced Wild Weasel prototypes, including 69-7254 (seen here on 23 January 1976). The 20mm cannon was removed from behind the radar, and that space and the gun trough under the nose radome were taken up by radiation sensors and ECM. F-4Gs can be distinguished from -Es by the extended and rounded chin fairing in place of the cannon's muzzle and by the enlarged tail-warning radar at the tip of the vertical fin. (USAF)

105▼

106. Another Advanced Wild Weasel prototype was used to test the new AGM-88A HARM (High-speed Anti-Radiation Missile) which is just now (late 1983) coming into service with the Air Force and Navy for use by F-4Gs and A-7s (and presumably by F-18s when they replace A-7s). Note the extended outboard leading-edge slats and the F-4E (the -G designation came later) Advanced Wild Weasel patch on the fuselage. (Texas Instruments)

107. A line-up of F-4Gs (tailcode 'WW') and F-4Es ('GA') of the 35th TFW at George AFB, during Exercise 'Coronet Spray', March 1981. Black tailcodes have generally replaced white (or pale grey) in all TAC units. Later F-4Gs can be identified by a cloverleaf-pattern sensor on the side of the chin sensor fairing. Note the wing badge on the fuselage of the nearest Phantom. (USAF)

106

107▼

▲108 ▼109

108. The 37th TFW, also based at George AFB, brought F-4Gs to Europe during Operation 'Reforger' in October 1982. Even with the sophisticated built-in electronics of the Wild Weasel, the aircraft often carry the ALQ-119 ECM pod as additional protection. (USAF)

109, 110. Two views of an F-4G (ex-F-4E, 68-582) of the 563rd TFS, 37th TFW, in front of a hardened shelter at RAF Wildenrath during 'Reforger 82'. This airframe obviously saw service over Vietnam, witness the trio of red stars on the splitter plate. (USAF)

110▼

▲111

111. One USAFE unit that has recently acquired F-4Gs is the 52nd TFW at Spangdahlem AB, West Germany. Note the 'SP' tailcode on this F-4G (ex-F-4E, 69-255), at RAF Greenham Common in 1980. The 52nd continues its tradition of experimenting with camouflages with this yellow-striped -G which uses brown in place of the dark green in its Vietnam-style finish. (J. Erwin Jose)

112. The Royal Navy contracted with McDonnell Aircraft for a pair of prototypes of F-4Js modified to British specifications. Most of the modifications were required by the adoption of Rolls-Royce Spey RB-168-25R Mk 202/203 turbofans in place of the standard J79s. The Speys were longer than the GE engines and required more airflow, necessitating a redesign of the engine inlet system. Other changes from the -J included a hinged radome, a longer nosewheel leg and reduced tailplane anhedral. The two YF-4Ks were followed by 50 production aircraft (British designation Phantom FG Mk 1). (McDonnell Douglas)

113. The Royal Air Force followed the RN order with a requirement for 118 F-4Ms (British designation Phantom FGR Mk 2), two prototypes (XT852 was the first YF-4M) and 116 production models. These differed from the -Ks in having a standard size nosewheel leg, no tailplane slots and modified avionics. Since the retirement of HMS *Ark Royal*, the remaining F-4Ks have been transferred to RAF control. (McDonnell Douglas)

112▲ 113▼

▲114

▲115

114. Not having an extensive reserve structure like the Air National Guard to absorb its ageing early Phantoms, the Navy has chosen to keep most of its F-4Bs in service by instituting a major modernization programme, such as that which the Air Force later set up for its F-4Es. The product of this upgrade was the F-4N, the example depicted belonging to VF-171's Key West Detachment and photographed at Andrews AFB. VF-171 has taken over from VF-101 as the Atlantic Fleet RAG squadron. Note the overall gull grey camouflage adopted by the Navy late in the 1970s. The lettering in the red, white and blue fuselage badge reads 'F-4N ACM VF-171'. (Dana Bell)
115. F-4Ns went to sea with VMFA-531 during the Iranian Crisis. A pair of 'Grey Ghosts' -Ns (BuNo 152323 in the foreground, 151477 on the port catapult) are being positioned for launch from *Coral Sea* in the Indian Ocean, March 1980. The Phantom nearest the camera is another CAG aircraft – note the 'Double Nuts' and multicolour rudder stripes. (US Navy)
116, 117, 118. The trend in US Navy camouflage and markings over the last decade has been towards less and less colour. These three views of F-4Ns of VMFA-321 show the early stages of that transition. In the mid 1970s, these Marine Phantoms were extremely colourful, with blue spine and tail with white stars and a red and white code. By the late 1970s nearly all the colour had gone, the 'MG' tailcode now being black. By the early 1980s, VMFA-321 had changed to the overall gull grey camouflage scheme and had incorporated a red pitchfork in its tail design, but all other markings, except for the national insignia and intake warning chevrons, were white. (Dana Bell)

MG
2303
VMFA-321
MARINES
9
VMFA-323
11

116▲

00
MG
2307
VMFA-321
MARINES
00

117▲ 118▼

MG
VMFA-321
1511
MARINES
134
VT-86
NAVY

▲119 ▼120

119, 120, 121. Another trio of views of F-4Ns, this time from VF-202 of the Naval Reserve based at NAS Dallas; reserve fighter units have now all switched over to N-model Phantoms. As late as April 1982, 'Superheats' Phantoms still carried full colours – a red, white and blue Lone Star flag of Texas on the rudder and a yellow and black diagonal fuselage stripe. Less than a year later, the same airframe is seen in the maintenance hangar, having lost the diagonal fuselage stripe. This F-4N, however, was the last of the colourful 'Superheats' Phantoms: the remaining aircraft on the flight-line look like '202', all markings now grey. Note the 'Battle E' for excellence in tactical skills and the 'S' for safety on the splitter plates. (Dana Bell)

121▼

▲122

123▲

122, 123. The final stage in the evolution of the Phantom's camouflage is shown in these views of F-4Ns of the other Naval Reserve squadron at NAS Dallas, the 'Hunters' of VF-201, March 1983. A few 'Hunters' Phantoms still are painted in relatively colourful markings over the gull grey scheme of the late 1970s, but most have now been repainted in a standard 'tactical' scheme adopted by the Navy after trials conducted by VF-103 and VF-171. This scheme uses three tones of grey : the two lighter colours are the same ghost grey tones used in F-15-style air superiority camouflages, and the darkest tone is a medium grey-blue. All markings are grey as well, either blue-grey over light grey or vice versa.

124. The Marine reserves also fly a squadron of F-4Ns out of NAS Dallas, and VMFA-112 is going through the same gradual transition in camouflage. In the foreground, BuNo 152310 is in the late 1970s scheme, whilst a squadron mate parked behind is in the new three-tone grey camouflage, March 1983.

◀124

125. The latest version of the 'Playboy Phantom' is an F-4S (BuNo 155539), seen here at NAS Dallas in March 1983, whither it had escorted a pair of VX-4's F-18 Hornets for ACM training.

CAPT. MIKE WELCH
DANGER
JET
INTAKE

▲126

126. Probably the last mark of the Phantom is the F-4S, such as BuNo 155767 of VF-171, at NAS Oceana on 19 April 1982. F-4Ss are upgraded F-4Js with manoeuvring slats on the wing leading edge. The Navy was reluctant to adopt these slats because they increased landing speeds (slats are less effective in generating lift than the older blown flaps), but was finally so impressed by the increased ACM capability brought by the slats that it was willing to accept any ancillary disadvantages. This Phantom was one of the dozen or so F-4s used to test the new tactical scheme. (Dana Bell)

127. Old Phantoms never die – they just gather dust (but not rust) at DoD's aircraft storage facility (MASDC, Military Aircraft Storage and Disposition Center) at Davis-Monthan AFB, Arizona. This F-4B (BuNo 151510), late of VF-111 'Sundowners', waits to be recalled; the chances are that this aircraft will fly again. Several nations have considered the Phantom obsolete and contemplated its retirement, but it still fli with every service that has ever purchased it (with the possible exception of Iran) and will probably do so for very many years t come.

127